ELEPHANTS

Wildlife Monographs - Elephants
Copyright © 2004 Evans Mitchell Books

Text and photography copyright © 2004 ARWP Ltd

Dr. Tracey Rich and Andy Rouse have asserted their rights
to be identified as the author and photographer of this work in
accordance with Section 77 of the Copyright, Designs and
Patents Act 1988

First published in Great Britain by
Evans Mitchell Books
Norfolk Court
1, Norfolk Road
Rickmansworth
Herts. WD3 1 LA
United Kingdom

Jacket and book design by
Sunita Gahir
Big Metal Fish Design Services
bigmetalfish.com

Maps by Mark Franklin

British Library Cataloguing in Publication Data. A CIP record of
this book is available on request from the British Library.

ISBN: 1-901268-08-X

10 9 8 7 6 5 4 3 2 1

Printed and bound in Hong Kong

ELEPHANTS

DR. TRACEY RICH & ANDY ROUSE

Evans Mitchell Books

CONTENTS

FOREWORD

THE AFRICAN ELEPHANT still roams freely in the majority of the countries of sub-Saharan Africa. Despite all the wars and conflicts, despite the rapid expansion of the human species into almost every nook and cranny of the continent, elephants have managed to hang on.

Sometimes, this is in vast areas within national parks; but more often simply living in places where they can simply find enough food, and increasingly in close contact with man. They cover magnificent expanses of natural habitat, from deserts to forests and from sea level to the snows of Kilimanjaro. In the savannahs, they are easiest to see and it is here in Samburu amongst other places around the globe that Andy Rouse and Tracey Rich have created the magnificent images of this book.

Every so often, there is something fresh and wonderful that meets the eye. Andy Rouse and Tracey Rich are photographers capable of finding new images of animals in new ways that have a novelty even on a subject as well covered as the elephant.

Having seen them work at first hand I realise this comes from immense patience, waiting for the right light and the right moment, and then having the expertise to capture behaviour in mid-flight. Elephants have captivated mankind through the ages, but for most of the world who cannot afford the a trip to see them in the wild the only way is it to look at the images of those who have travelled to the elephants' home. It is a miracle that they have survived so well since they are under threat from many quarters, including the would be ivory traders and the encroachment of agriculturalists into their land. If elephants are to survive into the future they need a constituency of human beings who wish them well. The ultimate determinant of their future will be human politics, and this is ruled by human sentiment. In this connection I hope that the images contained within this book will reach a wide audience and persuade new people to become elephant lovers and to take an interest in the survival of this species.

Dr Iain Douglas-Hamilton
Save the Elephants, Samburu NP, Kenya

INTRODUCTION

Elephants are probably the most recognisable and one of the most enigmatic creatures on Earth. The elephant is a curious creature evoking an unprecedented reaction in human beings together with what is often described as a strange empathy between man and wild animal. Whether this stems primarily from our fascination at its apparent strength and sheer size or from its strangely familiar behaviour and social structure, which is reminiscent of our own, this largest of land mammals has been and continues to be revered across societies and between cultures throughout the globe, even in areas where they sadly no longer exist in the wild.

This book will take you on a fascinating, albeit brief journey into the world of the elephant. Lavishly illustrated with stunning photographs by

RIGHT: Elephants are one of the most recognisable creatures on Earth. This family of Asian elephants, crossing a lake at sunrise, is no exception.

ABOVE: Juvenile Asian elephants enjoy playing in the shallow waters at sunset. Intelligent and sentient beings, elephants have a complex social structure based on families much like our own.

LEFT: The largest of terrestrial mammals, this African bull elephant is huge and part of a bachelor herd in Botswana.

highly skilled professional wildlife photographers, *Wildlife Monographs — Elephants* provides a highly privileged insight into the daily lives of elephants from various regions around the world - from wrinkled newborns to magnificently aggressive bulls and playful juveniles to the directed leadership of the matriarch. Join us as we explore the natural realm of the elephant and catch glimpses of their highly intriguing and endlessly fascinating lives.

HISTORY & DISTRIBUTION

Elephants have been roaming the Earth for many millions of years before humans. Modern day elephants are descended from a group of prehistoric animals termed 'the mastodons' (meaning 'big toothed/tusked'), which included woolly mammoths.

Elephants have roamed the earth for many millions of years. Scenes like these will have changed little in all of that time.

LEFT: Asian elephants are found in lush tropical areas. They like nothing more than to bathe in the refreshing lakes and rivers.

LEFT AND BELOW: Once covering habitats from sub-Saharan Africa through to China, the elephants' range has fragmented in response to the expansion of the human population and its effects on the environment.

Fossil records from Africa have dated the mastodons to around the middle Eocene period, between 54 to 38 million years ago. To put this into context, the earliest human fossil recorded dates from approximately 100 thousand years ago. Evolutionary studies have shown that elephants are related to some very curious creatures still in existence today, including the rock hyrax (*Procavia johnstoni*), a small furry rodent living in rocky outcrops of the African savannah.

In the twenty-first century we have two scientifically recognised separate species of elephant, the African elephant (*Loxodonta africana*) and Asian elephant (*Elaphus maximus*). Relatively recently, a third type of elephant was discovered, the African forest-dwelling elephant (*Loxodonta cyclotis*) which is now thought by experts to be a completely separate species. The forest elephant has been seldom observed although scientific research is now underway in order to determine more about it and its needs in order that we may conserve them.

ABOVE: There are three scientifically recognised species of elephant; the African, Asian and forest-dwelling African elephant.

In the past, elephants have been a common natural feature around the globe. They were ubiquitous throughout sub-Saharan Africa and throughout Asia, from the Tigris-Euphrates river system in the west, through Asia south of the Himalayas and east to China. Today, the range and numbers have shrunk with the expansion of human population and associated effects such as habitat destruction and ivory poaching.

The Asian elephant remains scattered in isolated populations within its former range, from southern India and Sri Lanka, through to parts of eastern China and south to Indonesia and Malaysia.

In Africa, in the early 1980s, it was estimated that around 1.3 million

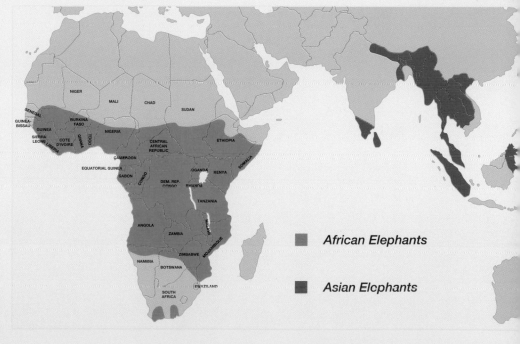

African Elephants

Asian Elephants

LEFT: An elderly Asian bull elephant. He is a symbol of what was once a population of several hundreds of thousands of elephants, but which is now an endangered species.

ABOVE: The population of African savannah-dwelling elephants was decimated by ivory poaching during the 1980s. Today, with special protection measures in place, the population is recovering. Note the baby elephant, which is only a few days old.

ABOVE RIGHT: Long-lived animals such as elephants need special protection and management in order to retain sufficient numbers to safeguard a sustainable breeding population.

elephants roamed the existing wilderness areas. Today, this figure is around 400,000. Across Asia, at the beginning of the 20th century, it has been estimated that there were in excess of 100,000 Asian elephants. Now, this figure is thought to be in the region of 35,000 to 54,000 remaining in the wild. Man's activity, including the lucrative trade in ivory has caused both the African and Asian elephant to become officially 'endangered' according to IUCN (International Union for Nature Conservation) status classification. Accordingly, both species are listed under Appendix I of the 1973 Convention on International Trade in Endangered Species of Wild Flora and Fauna (CITES).

DISTINGUISHING FEATURES

ELEPHANTS

Today elephants hold the record for being the largest land mammal on Earth. They are long-lived, up to 60-70 years of age, and weigh in at an impressive average 5000kg (about 11,000lb) for a mature African male (bull) elephant – equivalent to about 80 people – with the female (cow) at around 3000kg (over 6,500lb). Asian elephants weights are in a similar range to those of African elephants. However, forest elephants weigh between 1800 – 3200kg (4,000 – 7,000lb).

Bull elephants stand at over 3m (10ft) tall, with 2.5m for a cow. Interestingly, the highest point of an African elephant is its shoulder, whereas in Asian elephants it is the top of its head. The Asian elephant is generally a little smaller in stature compared to its African counterpart and has a more leggy and rounded appearance. The forest elephant is described as being considerably smaller than the savannah-dwelling African elephant, standing at around 2.6m (8.5ft) tall.

ABOVE AND BELOW: Elephants are awesome creatures whatever way you look at them.

RIGHT: A sexually receptive Asian bull strides out across the plain in search of females.

LEFT, RIGHT, ABOVE & BELOW: The elephant's trunk is one of the most useful appendages in the animal kingdom. Here, you can see just how flexible and adaptable it is, being used for feeding, touching, holding, grasping, showering, bathing , drinking, smelling and dusting — just a few of its uses.

TRUNK

OF COURSE, the main distinguishing feature of an elephant is its trunk. A form of elongated nose, the trunk is prehensile in nature being able to grip and hold things much like a hand, as well as serving a multitude of other purposes. Fully extendable, the trunk contains in the region of 4,000 muscles. With such a prominent nasal appendage, it is unsurprising that elephants have an amazing sense of smell. In addition to this, the trunk can also be used for other forms of communication such as signalling and touching, as well as their most noticeable functions of feeding and drinking. The trunk can allow the elephant to reach anywhere from ground level up to 6m high. In the Asian elephant, the trunk has a distinctive, single finger-like projection on the upper tip. This is used for grasping and clutching, as well as delicate touching. In contrast, the African elephant trunk has an additional finger on the lower tip of the trunk as well. The elephant's trunk is a unique appendage and one that has served it well, helping elephants to exploit existing different habitat types and to adapt to ever-changing man-made pressures both upon the species themselves and their environment.

TUSKS

FLANKING EACH side of the trunk, elephants have large tusks that gently curve upwards. These appear both in males and females in African elephants but are often absent from Asian elephants. Instead, females in particular may have small 'tushes', which are seldom visible. The forest elephants of central Africa generally have tusks that point downwards. Tusks are made of ivory similar to the material that makes up our own teeth. Tusks are used for many purposes including digging, fighting and general leverage: sometimes this leads to worn or broken tusks. Another point of interest is that elephants, like ourselves, can be biased towards the left or right-hand side. As a result of such bias, elephants will often be seen to have one tusk that is worn or somewhat shorter than the other.

THIS PAGE: Tusks too are very useful tools and occasionally weapons. They generally increase in size with advancing age.

RIGHT: Elephants can be right or left tusked, much as we can be right- or left-handed. Note the worn tusk of this mother.

LEFT: A desert-dwelling elephant in Namibia has worn tusks. He uses these to dig for scarce water resources.

RIGHT: An elephant's tusks continue to grow throughout its life. Here, a juvenile shows off his small but perfectly formed pair.

As a general rule male elephants have larger tusks than females. They grow continuously throughout an elephant's life and normally get bigger with age. The tusks of mature African bull elephants can even reach up to 3.4m (some 11ft) in length and weigh 61kg (135lb).

The size of an elephant's tusks is mainly genetically controlled: that is to say, that an elephant born to, or sired by, an elephant with big tusks is likely itself to have big tusks when fully mature. The genetic influence on tusk growth may be seen in the absence of ivory-carrying Asian elephants. Tuskless elephants may reflect the intensity of ivory poaching. The number of Asian elephants with tusks varies dramatically between regions, from 90 per cent in southern India to 5 per cent in Sri Lanka.

EARS

ELEPHANTS HAVE very large ears and these enormous ear flaps, positioned on either side of the head, are vitally important to them. Ear flaps provide a large surface area form which excess heat can escape, as well as signalling moods and intentions to others. Unsurprisingly, elephants have exceptionally good hearing. With ears measuring in the region of 2m (6.5ft) by 1.5m (5ft) they are some of the largest in the animal kingdom. The size of an elephant's ears are another distinguishing feature between elephant types. African elephants have the largest ears, which are chiefly rounded in shape. An Asian elephant's ears are much smaller, less rigid and more triangular in shape; and forest elephants are reported to have oval-shaped ears.

LEFT, ABOVE AND BELOW: The difference between African and Asian elephants is very noticeable from their ears. Asian elephants (above) have smaller, less rigid ears with less venation. African elephant ears are larger, squarer and with greater venation to dissipate heat gained from the scorching African sun.

HEAD

SMALL BEADY eyes set high on the head lead experts to believe that elephant eyesight is not as acute as their other senses. Elephants are believed to be able to see clearly up to 10m (38ft) away and they see best under dim light conditions around dawn and dusk — when they require a little extra vigilance as potential predators are likely to be hunting.

The shape of an elephant's head is also a good indicator of elephant species. The African elephant tends to have a generally squarer head than the Asian species, whose head has distinctive domed lobes and a generally more rounded appearance.

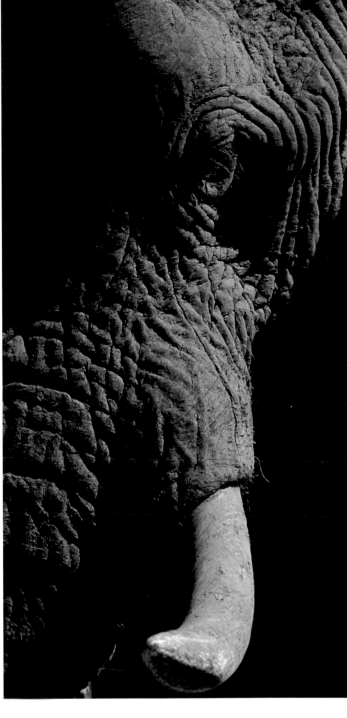

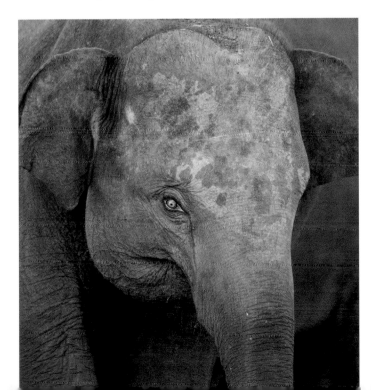

LEFT: An Asian elephant has a distinctively lobed head.

ABOVE: Small eyes suggest that an elephant's eyesight is not as well developed as its other senses.

FEET

THE FEET of an elephant are surprisingly sensitive. They are used not only for locomotion but also as a tool: to kick up potential food items, such as grasses and tubers, and for manipulating objects in conjunction with the trunk. The sensitivity of the feet means that an elephant may use them to investigate novel objects or to check the terrain to assess whether a place is safe to cross. When observing elephants, it also becomes clear that feet are used in tactile communication between individuals. especially during play in youngsters.

Elephant species can be distinguished by their feet. Asian elephants have four toenails on their fore and hind feet whereas African elephants only have three toenails on their rear feet. Strangely, the forest elephant is described as having five toenails on the fore feet and four on the rear.

SKIN

AN ELEPHANT'S SKIN is dry, thick and grey. Deeply wrinkled and textured: an elephant's skin can be in the region of 3 cm thick. Despite this, the skin is well supplied with nerves and bristly hairs and is, therefore, pliable and very sensitive to touch. Consequently, elephants take great care of their skin, protecting it from the harsh effects of the sun by bathing and coating it in mud or dust. Many elephants appear brown or even red in colouration depending upon the composition of the local soil. Asian elephant skin is often less pigmented than that of its African relatives and where pigment is lacking can appear pink in colouration. Furthermore, Asian elephants are noticeably hairy when young, gradually becoming less so with increasing age.

LEFT: Elephant feet are important in feeding as well as locomotion and are used in conjunction with the trunk.

ABOVE AND RIGHT: Sensitive and pliable: an elephant takes great care of its skin, bathing regularly and protecting it from the harsh effects of the sun and skin parasites by coating it liberally in mud or dust.

LOCOMOTION

ELEPHANTS MOVE in a very distinctive manner; their gait is an ambling walk, which simply increases in speed and stride length when covering distances in haste. Their normal walking speed is between 6 and 8kph (approximately 4-5mph). When charging an elephant can reach speeds of up to 30kph (approximately 18mph), which is far faster than humans can run.

For their immense size and considerable bulk, elephants are particular agile and can climb steep slopes very well. When descending they will frequently resort to sliding on their haunches. They are also capable of standing erect on their hind legs in order to reach food and this position is also adopted by male elephants during mating.

RIGHT: Elephants can move with great agility and speed for their size. They use traditional tracks to navigate through their environment, the details of which are passed from one generation to another.

HABITAT & DIET

For their size, elephants have been extremely adaptable in their colonisation and use of a diverse variety of habitat types; from montane forests to lowland swamps, and from savannah woodland to desert. In fact, the main parameters governing where an elephant can live are simply that it has to have an adequate food and water supply. Dietary requirements dictate that an elephant's diet is varied. Many different types of grasses and browse (for example, leaves and tree bark) are eaten according to the season; and elephants select those which are the most nutritious and in plentiful supply at any particular time. Elephant movements throughout their range are consequently determined largely by the nutritional value and abundance of their food at different times of year. They will often move to areas where there has recently been localised rainfall.

LEFT: Elephants spend in the region of 16 hours a day feeding and it is an important social activity.

Being the largest land mammal and with a diet that is nutritionally poor (relative to other mammals) means that elephants have enormous appetites and spend most of their day foraging, usually around 16 hours a day. These periods of feeding activity occur throughout the day interspersed with periods of rest when elephants find a cool place in the shade away from the harsh sun to digest their food and snooze. Adult elephants tend to sleep for about 4-5 hours in a day, most of the rest of the time taken up with other social activities. An elephant needs to eat on average 4 to 6 per cent of its body weight in food per day, which is surprisingly little for such a large herbivore.

Needless to say, having eaten all of that food, elephants produce some of the largest dung in the animal kingdom. This dung consists of undigested vegetable matter and an elephant can excrete

LEFT, ABOVE AND RIGHT: Elephant diets are diverse and seasonal. They select carefully the most nutritious and palatable foods in their environment and harvest these in a sustainable manner.

LEFT: This African elephant clearly demonstrates the delicacy with which it can use its trunk for feeding from this acacia tree.

RIGHT: In the heat of the day, elephants will rest in the shade to digest their food and sleep.

BELOW: Grazing or browsing, elephants are adaptable in their use of food resources.

around 155kg (350lb) a day. They do this by passing faeces three to five times in the space of approximately an hour and a half. Elephant dung would soon build up into huge mountains if it were not for the small creatures that utilise it. Dung beetles rely upon elephant dung and are specialised at recycling it. By rolling small boluses away, the beetles help to dissipate the enormous mounds of accumulating dung throughout the habitat and make it available for plants to use. It is odd to think that some of the very smallest creatures in the world are dependent upon some of the very largest animals on the planet and vice-versa. These special relationships are especially pertinent in desert areas where the moisture contained within elephant dung is often a life-saving commodity to plants and animals alike.

Water is one of the most vital components of elephant life. They consume in the region of 227ltrs (60gal) a day and a mature bull can drink up to 100 litres (26gal) in one sitting. Elephants usually trav-

RIGHT: Elephants are big eaters and produce copious amounts of dung. Here, a bull elephant inspects a dunging area or 'midden' where he can collect information about others from this smelly notice board.

BELOW: Dung beetles are reliant upon elephant dung and elephants depend upon dung beetles to process their waste and fertilise the plants in their habitat.

OVERLEAF: Elephants in semi-arid conditions are reliant on scarce water resources, so they must visit them regularly. Here, we can see a herd from the air.

LEFT: In times of plenty, elephants will feed almost continuously but their need for water means that will range up to 10km a day in search of it.

RIGHT: Water is an essential component of elephant life and dictates where it is able to live.

BELOW: In desert areas, elephants, like this solitary bull will dig for water and vital minerals such as those containing sodium.

el about 10km (6miles) per day, but may sometimes walk 30 km (18 miles) or more. In arid areas elephants will walk up to 80 km (50 miles) a day in search of water. Elephants of the Namibian deserts are specialised at seeking water located underground, beneath dried-up riverbeds. They use their tusks and trunks to excavate wells where they can quench their thirsts and gather scarce minerals and salts from the soils and rocks that are missing from their meagre diet. This process also makes the water and minerals available to other animals that otherwise would not be able to access them. Sodium is the main element that is often lacking from elephant diets in harsh environments. The desire for this mineral is so strong that elephants have been known to climb mountain slopes and enter deep into caves in order to search out this precious mineral.

Elephants need a large 'home range' to find enough food and water for their needs. Depending

on the peculiarities of the habitat, proximity of humans and resource abundance, elephant home ranges may be anything from 3000 to 3500 sq km (1,100 – 1,350 sq miles). It is believed that prior to human intervention, many elephants were chiefly migratory, a tendency still seen today. They traverse their home range periodically and follow traditional 'elephant paths' to migrate from one area to another. African elephants are predominantly savannah dwelling, hence their greater adaptations for heat loss (e.g. large ears and flapping behaviour) and dependence on localised water resources. On the other hand, Asian elephants and the forest elephants of Africa are generally forest and woodland dwellers thus do not have such a need for excessive heat loss or such a dependence on local water sources.

PREVIOUS: Elephants love water and may drink up to 227 litres (60 gallons) a day. Here, a Sri Lankan elephant family quench their thirsts.

LEFT AND ABOVE: Elephant home ranges can be between 3000 and 3,500 sq km (bout 1100 to1350 sq miles). They have a tendency to be migratory within these areas following localised rainfall.

SOCIAL STRUCTURE & COMMUNICATION

Elephants are often described as being highly social animals, meaning that they tend to prefer to live with members of the same species - and specifically within family groups, much as we do. Elephant society is based on extended families. Family herds consist mostly of related females - sisters, daughters, cousins and their offspring.

A group of elephants is led by the matriarch, usually the most dominant older female in the herd. The matriarch dictates how and when the family moves, rests, drinks and feeds. She is responsible for the co-ordination of the herd and the protection of young. The matriarch's knowledge of the home range and traditionally-used water sources is vital to the herd's success and survival. She gains this knowledge not only from life experience (vital to such a long-lived animal) but also through information passed on to her from her mother and other family members.

RIGHT: The social bonds between individuals in an elephant herd are strong.

48

LEFT: Elephants have an intricate knowledge of their home range and will be led by the matriarch along traditional 'elephant paths'.

ABOVE: Each herd member is responsible for the welfare of youngsters. Here, family members take care of a baby whilst drinking on the river's edge.

The size of an elephant group can vary considerably, from around three to 30 individuals plus their offspring. However, an average family consists of around 10 individual female elephants. Groups that become too large usually divide into two but remain in close contact with each other, often spending about half their time still together. Families also have close association with other groups, collectively known as 'bond groups' or 'clans'. Bond groups usually stay in close contact (within a mile or two of each other) and can consist of two or three families. Highly excitable greetings

PREVIOUS: Families are important to Asian elephants too.
Here, a mix of age groups happily feed together after sunset.

are known to take place when these groups meet, even after fairly short periods of absence.

Many social activities and interactions occur between elephants around water sources, such as on river banks, lake edges and at waterholes. Where vital resources such as water are restricted, a strict hierarchy of access is established. It is the matriarch who determines who drinks when and where. Bathing, mud bathing and dusting are vitally important parts of an elephant's daily routine. An elephant can survive several days without water, but given a choice will drink and bathe everyday.

Elephants appear to enjoy bathing in mud and water, wallowing in the shallows and even completely submerging themselves in deeper water. Even newborn elephants are taken straight into water and can swim from their first day. Showering, using the trunk, will occur when water is too shallow in which to wallow; and mothers will often assist young by showering and scrubbing them with their trunks. Following bathing, elephants will often continue their grooming routine by rubbing themselves against rocks and

RIGHT: Bath time for elephants is an important social activity whether this be wallowing in water, mud or dust.

54

LEFT, ABOVE AND RIGHT:
' ...there's nothing quite like it for cooling the blood…', elephants use bathing as a means of cooling themselves, maintaining their skin in good condition and free from parasite infection as well as for socialising with others.

Samburu National Park, Kenya.

It is the matriarch of the family herd who decides when and where the herd goes. After four hours of moving to and fro and a couple of aborted crossing attempts, this matriarch had finally decided that the conditions were right for the herd to cross the swollen river in order to reach fresh feeding grounds. In the process of crossing the elephants had to swim, using their trunks as a form of snorkel. The power of the river swept a young baby downstream away from the safe crossing point and the rest of the herd.

Amazingly, instead of saving themselves and striving to reach safety of the other bank, the whole herd swam as fast as they could downstream after the lost baby, who by this time was barely visible above the torrent of muddy water. Upon reaching the baby, they surrounded it, forming a type of elephant raft. Gradually, together, they steered themselves towards the bank. This was about a kilometre from where they had set out. The baby, clinging onto a herd member's trunk with its own, and with a few more inelegant shoves from various other trunks belonging to aunties and cousins, was safely upon dry land again - a little shaken but none the worse for its ordeal. A frenzy of trumpeting by the herd members echoed across the plains for half-an-hour or so; and then all was quiet again as the elephants got back to munching their favourite palm trees.

ABOVE: Crossing this river was usually uneventful but due to recent rains even elephants found it hard going — losing a young baby downstream in the process!

BELOW: Some of the family wait nervously, mustering courage to cross the river.

trees. The same locations are used frequently, causing the trunks of some trees to become rubbed smooth and highly polished by the persistent use.

Elephants are sentient beings and they have complex forms of communication that are vital to maintain cohesion and co-ordination of the extended family. Elephants are renown for their complex repertoire of vocalisations: many of these are made in the infra-sound range of the sound spectrum, (a frequency around 14hz and at levels up to 103 decibels) and well below the threshold of human hearing. Vocalisations are known to signify a wide range of emotional states. Elephants can be described as rumbling, moaning, growling, bellowing, trumpeting and screaming, to name just some of their noises.

Elephants use a combination of acoustic, tactile, chemical and visual signals to communicate between each other under different social contexts. Strong emotional bonds and effective forms of communication between individual elephants are known to be important in reassuring youngsters,

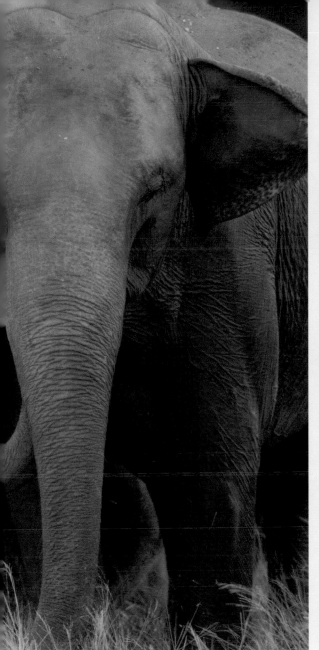

LEFT, ABOVE AND RIGHT:

Communication between elephants
is a complex affair involving touch,
sound, sight, taste and smell.
Elephants have a large repertoire
of behaviours, indicating a variety
of emotional states. Note that this
matriarch has been fitted with a
radio-collar.

LEFT: Smell is an important sense to elephants as they maintain constant contact with each other over vast distances, using sounds and scents in particular.

ABOVE AND RIGHT: Youngsters learn directly from their mothers. Knowledge and skills are acquired through strong social bonds and communication between individuals.

reconciling differences between individuals, in forming coalitions with other groups against aggressors and for keeping in touch with family members over long distances.

BELOW AND RIGHT: Male (bull) elephants lead reasonably solitary lives compared to females. Some may join bachelor herds until they are mature enough to become successful sires.

LEFT: Males are tolerated with the family group until they reach sexual maturity.

ABOVE: As solitary bull displaying aggression at an unusual object (this time the photographer approaching the river bank in a canoe!)

Male and female elephants lead dissimilar lives. Male elephants are tolerated within the herd until sexual maturity when they will either join bachelor herds or live a relatively solitary lifestyle, loosely following female herds but ranging more widely. Bachelor herds number between two and 14 individuals and are comprised of a mixture of age groups.

REPRODUCTION

ELEPHANTS

Elephants become sexually mature at 12 years of age. They do not specifically have a breeding season, but breeding activity often coincides with seasonal rains. At this time, a great many families may congregate, sometimes consisting of upwards of 100 individuals. This is when mature bull elephants also join the aggregation. Although not territorial, male elephants do compete for dominance over access to females and this is when they can become very aggressive.

Mating success with the receptive females – thus becoming the sire of the next generation of elephants - is dependent upon this aggression, physical size and weapons (tusks). Males spend much time testing each other's strength by wrestling. This aggression can sometimes escalate to chases and physical combat when the competitors are equally matched. The most dominant (and senior, around 35+ years of age) bull elephants usually secure the most successful mating attempts, although younger bulls may be encouraged by females to mate with them. This is likely to be a means of ensuring that the most dominant bulls are attracted to the females, whilst allowing the younger bulls to gain experience and form

LEFT: Bull elephants that are the most dominant usually have greater mating success.

ABOVE: Similarly matched bulls may spar and even fight to assert dominant and mating rights. Here, the loser of a sparring match is chased away by the victor.

LEFT: Bull elephants may become aggressive during musth.

BELOW: Two Asian elephants, both in musth, eye each other to assess dominance and access to receptive females.

relationships with the females - which may be useful in successful breeding attempts in the future.

When male elephants are sexually active, they are often said to be in 'musth', a condition peculiar to elephants. The most obvious signs of musth in a male elephant is a distinctive oozing of fluid from the temporal glands located on either side of the head, and the continuous dripping of fluid from the penis. These secretions have a pungent odour. A male elephant in musth also tends to become highly aggressive and from a potential competitor's (and human) perspective it is at its most dangerous,

as the individual is likely to react unpredictably and charge. Female elephants prefer to mate with males in musth.

In Asian elephants the temporal gland is only active in males in a state of sexual arousal. Unusually, in African elephant males and females secrete from their temporal glands at times of excitement or anxiety. This has led to the belief that the response is related to the release of adrenaline or testosterone into the blood stream. In African elephants, the onset of temporal gland activity occurs during infancy; so the full significance of this reaction remains unclear.

ABOVE: Temporal gland secretions in male and female African elephants begins in infancy.

RIGHT: Bull elephants can detect receptive females some way away by their scent (sex pheromones). Sparring between bull elephants escalates at sexual maturity.

ABOVE AND RIGHT: Baby elephants suckle from mammary glands located between the forelegs of its mother.

Mating itself is a rather awkward affair and involves a complex courtship ritual. This consists of a female approaching a bull, backing up to him, allowing him to test her for oestrus by sniffing her genitalia with his trunk and tasting her secretions. The pair may walk together for several hours, sometimes this will break into chase. Finally, the female will permit the bull to mount her, copulation lasting around 45 seconds.

The period of gestation in elephants is around 22 months. A new-born calf weighs around 120kg (265lb). Calves are quick to get to their feet. It takes about 20 minutes for a calf to stand, from which time the calf becomes inseparable from its mother. The mother – calf bond remains for life. The calf

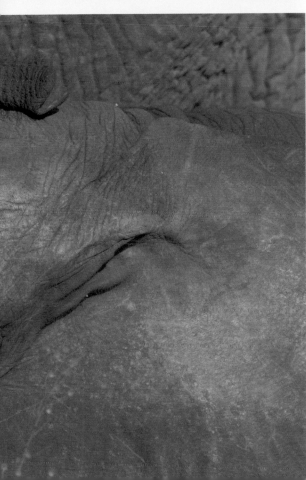

suckles from mammary glands located between the mother's forelegs and continues to suckle until 2-3 years old when it is weaned. Calves may continue to nurse from time to time for a couple of years following this. Due to the close knit community relationships of the elephant, calves may cross suckle with aunts or close relatives. All members of the family herd are responsible for looking after youngsters and to help educate them in elephant etiquette.

ELEPHANT WATCHING

Minneria National Park, Sri Lanka

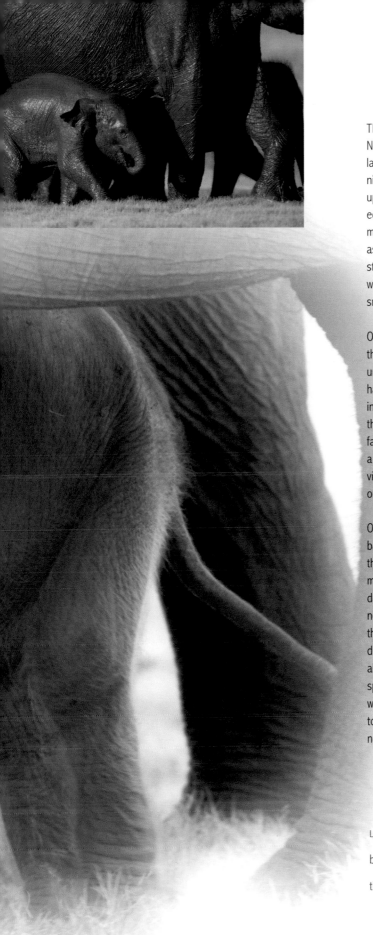

The matriarch of this group of Asian elephants in Minneria National Park, Sri Lanka had led her family down to the lakeside to drink and bathe in the last few hours before nightfall. Her family was one of many to be there that evening, upwards of 100 individuals were dispersed around the water's edge. The herd looked rather nervous as, tentatively, they made their way, munching the lush grasses on the flood plains as they went towards the enticing fresh water. Something was stirring amongst the herd. Juveniles were skittish and aunts were on the alert, frequently turning to raise their trunks and sniff the air.

Occasional trumpeting and rumblings were clearly audible and the group bunched tightly together, wheeling around at any unusual noise or movement. A few interested bulls were hanging around on the periphery of the group, some dripping in musth and on the search for receptive females. But surely that was not the cause of such concern in this particular family? Then the reason was revealed. Amongst the hubbub, a small wrinkled pink elephant with bright blue eyes was clearly visible between the legs of one of the females. It was unsteady on its feet and on first glance appeared unwell.

On closer inspection however, it was obvious that the baby elephant was fine, its appearance simply the result of having arrived in the world a matter of hours earlier, the umbilical cord still dangling from its middle. But having a new-born in tow was not going to deter this family from its daily ritual of drinking and bathing as they - along with the new-born - splashed happily into the water, baby sinking right up to its trunk as if it were nothing out of the ordinary.

LEFT: A baby Asian elephant born earlier in the day remains a little dazed and disorientated.

PREVIOUS: Mothers and aunts are responsible for teaching youngsters elephant etiquette. Here, a female physically reprimands an over-enthusiastic youngster.

LEFT, ABOVE AND RIGHT: Baby elephants of all kinds are adorable. Ungainly and awkward, they like nothing more than playing with their relatives and other herd members.

OVERLEAF: Playing is so tiring.

GROWING UP

Mother elephants will direct their young, often by steering them by their tails, helping them over obstacles, caressing them in times of anxiety, playing and reprimanding them with a slap or kick should they become too boisterous. Young calves like nothing more than playing, and older juveniles of different age classes provide vital playmates with whom to spar, wrestle and generally have fun with.

Youngsters learn by example and those being born to more dominant individuals automatically inheriting a higher position in the family hierarchy. They are quick to examine novel objects and to investigate new smells and tastes. Locations where groups of elephants regularly defecate, also called 'middens' are examined closely by all individuals and for youngsters must provide an important learning resource. Urine and faeces provide a type of smelly notice board where all of the latest news of individuals passing the area will be posted.

Protection of young is the responsibility of all family members. Individuals collectively will rally around to defend young from potential threats and predators such as lions. A typical defensive position being to form an outwardly facing circle

ABOVE: Siblings and playmates are important parts of a calf's upbringing and in the development social bonds, as these two in Sri Lanka show.

around the young secreted in the middle. To cross an area of potential danger, a family herd will move with the young in the middle of the group and will hurry to reach safety.

The strong bond between members of the family group is clearly illustrated by a family known as 'The Biblical Towns' living in Samburu National

ABOVE: An African youngster exploring the use of its trunk.

RIGHT: New born elephants remain close to their mothers who are on hand to lend a helping trunk to the situation.

Park in Kenya and studied by researchers from *Save the Elephants* organisation (see p88). Babul was born with a crippled hind leg. Incapable of placing any weight on this leg, she hops along on her remaining three good legs. Understandably, three legs are not as fast as four, so Babul will often be left behind as the group moves on to fresh feeding grounds. One would naturally predict that she would struggle to survive and be in danger of predation. However, 14 years later, Babul is still very much part of the Biblical Towns group of elephants. They will slow up to allow her to catch up with them as they move or actively return to find her should she be unable to keep up.

At the other end of the age spectrum, elephants survive long beyond their reproductive life span. This is most unusual and humans are the only other other mammal to do this regularly. A matriarch will usually end her reproductive life at around 45 years of age. Eventually, due to severe old age or infirmity, the matriarch will defer to a younger, more dominant female relative and remain on the periphery of the group or be extricated from the family group to survive alone until death.

ABOVE: Asian elephants have traditionally been used for logging in remote areas.

MAN & ELEPHANTS

The relationship between people and the elephant has been well documented over the centuries. A lasting fascination with this most enigmatic of creatures has led us to harness their immense power and strength for our own needs through domestication. Asian elephants in particular are known to be amenable to domestication, most frequently seen in entertainment (circuses and tourism) and zoological parks.

In India and other parts of Asia, people have had a strong working relationship with elephants for over 4,000 years. Rock paintings from many areas around the world depict forms of elephant, suggesting that their range persisted further than many biological records suggest. Elephants were even used by the Romans in warfare and by Hannibal in his adventures. Elephants have traditionally been used in tree-felling and for other hard, physical work in demanding areas.

The deep significance we have afforded to the elephant has been immortalised in many different religions, most notably in the form of the God Ganesh in Hindu and Buddhist faiths. The elephant has come to symbolise good, strength, honesty, generosity and power - to name but a few of its associated qualities. The elephant is a strong feature of religious architecture, being depicted in carvings and statues throughout the world.

ABOVE: Asian elephant taking part in religious festival.

Throughout Asia, many festivals are dedicated to elephants and elephant gods. In Sri Lanka, for example, elephants form a vitally important part of temple pageants and are given the responsibility of carrying sacred Buddhist relics. Each and every elephant is important to the procession that will wind its way around the town, visiting the temples in the vicinity. Many hours are spent grooming and bathing the animals in preparation for the procession and they are dressed in specifically designed costumes, intricately embroidered with mirrors and jewels. The elephants are further adorned with lights and often garlands of flowers and tusk covers made from gold and precious stones. The elephants are required to attend the temple physically in order to 'pray' in advance of the parade. It is yet another example of the belief that elephants are sentient beings, with their own thoughts and feelings.

These domesticated elephants not only have an important role to play in the daily lives of people and their religions, but are ambassadors for the rest of their kind. In having physical contact with elephants and being able to appreciate them at close proximity, people can foster an understanding of the animal and the need to protect and conserve its cousins in the wild areas of their countries.

RIGHT: Elephants appear in carvings and religious architecture around the world.

By giving each other mutual respect, in the past, humans and elephants have managed to co-exist happily and relatively peacefully throughout the globe.

However, with dwindling natural habitat and food resources alongside burgeoning human settlements, elephants are forced into closer and closer proximity to people. It is unsurprising, therefore, that given a choice between poorly nutritious and inadequate quantities of fodder in the remnants of the animal's natural habitat, that the elephant has learned to exploit the highly palatable and plentiful supplies of crops such as millet or paddy grown by Man. Elephants are highly intelligent animals and have learned to exploit crops planted adjacent to

their natural habitats, even becoming specialists at crop raiding in time.

People have to resort to physical force to drive the elephants away which in turn makes the elephants more aggressive towards them. Sometimes, people are killed by marauding elephants leading to localised culls of troublesome herds. Villages may resort to the erection of expensive electrified fences to protect their crops but even these are breached eventually, when elephant learns that the fence does not hurt them if they use their tusks or that their feet feel little of the fence's current. Some have even taken to charging the fence to gain access to the crops.

Ivory poaching has been another cause of imbalance in the human–elephant relationship in recent times, decimating the elephant populations of Asia and, in particular, Africa in the 1980s when the trade was at its peak, and the price of ivory approaching \$100/kg. By the early 1990s nearly 80% of the elephants in Central and eastern Africa had been wiped out. Thanks to world-wide concern over this dramatic drop in elephant numbers a ban on ivory trading was eventually reached and thanks to conservation efforts elephant numbers

RIGHT: Here, a scientific researcher uses radio telemetry to monitor elephants' habitat use and behaviour. Researcher image used larger please

are gradually beginning to recover. Scientific research into the lives of elephants has sought to bring greater understanding to the needs of elephants and how we may deal with the human-elephant relationship in the future.

Most information pertaining to the lives and requirements of elephants has come from direct observations and radio-tracking. Radio-collars are fitted to elephants when temporarily tranquilised. These give off a signal which can be detected via an antenna and box of electronics. Today, we can pinpoint individuals to specific locations utilising satellite technology and the global positioning system (GPS). The position of the elephant can thus be monitored. Also, with the addition of behavioural observations, much information can be gleaned their general ecology and how elephant groups react to changes in the environment. Knowledge is power, and this information can allow us to predict how elephants will react to specific situations, as well as providing an early warning system for potential problems.

In order that this information is used to the best possible outcome for both humans and elephants, people living alongside elephants need

to have the desire to conserve them in a manageable and sustainable way. Through community education projects many elephant conservation charities have become the catalyst to local elephant conservation and in fostering the mutual respect for Man and elephant which has been lacking in recent times.

A prime example is the work of the *Save the Elephants* organisation (www.savetheelephants.org), based in Kenya, East Africa. STE is a conservation charity born from the life-long research of African elephants by Dr Iain Douglas-Hamilton (who began his research in the late 1960's with a pioneering study of African elephants at Lake Manyara, Tanzania).

91

The charity was founded in 1993 and has a holistic approach to elephant conservation. STE focuses on four main areas of elephant conservation;

1) Scientific research of elephant ecology around the world,

2) Education of the needs of elephants and elephant conservation issues,

3) Local community based projects for those who live alongside elephants in the wild,

4) Protection of elephant populations by surveying to measure changes in response to the ivory trade.

STE supports a total ban on the ivory trade and believes that the trade itself is the greatest threat to elephant survival. The charity is recognised as an international organisation by CITIES and has been instrumental in finding new and unique methods of conserving elephants, including green hunting. Green hunting is a non-lethal sporting activity in which elephant conservation can be carried out in an economically and ethically sustainable way. It involves the darting of elephants for the purposes of collecting scientific information whilst providing paying clients with supreme sport hunting and acquisition of sporting trophies in the form of casts of the anaesthetised elephant's tusks.

It is in the support of such organisations and their activities that we can influence the future of elephant species most effectively and ensure that their populations remain for generations to come. The world would be a much poorer place with the loss of such wondrous and awesome animals. Their fate remains our responsibility and it is up to us to ensure that the joy and marvel of these creatures remains for the benefit of our natural world and those of us still to come.

Save the Elephants - Mission Statement:
"It is our mission to secure a future for elephants and to sustain the beauty and ecological integrity of the places where they live; to promote man's delight in their intelligence and the diversity of their world, and to develop a tolerant relationship between the two species".

RIGHT: African and Asian elephants deserve our support in order that these magnificent creatures and their natural habitats remain for future generations.

LEFT: The result of an aggressive elephant in musth on a researcher's vehicle. Fortunately the occupants survived — just.

ACKNOWLEDGEMENTS & INFORMATION

A great many people deserve specific thanks for their help in the production of this book including PVV and Prof. T, Iain and Oria Douglas-Hamilton, Gavin and Marjorie Blair, Andrew Momberg, Isaack Ntari, Ifham Raji, Kingsley Perera, Lalith Fernando at SriLankan Airlines, Greg and Wendy Trollip, the researchers at STE, Faisz Mustapha, the Sri Lanka Department of Wildlife Conservation, Steve Rouse, Sunita Gahir and of course the subjects of this book, the elephants, without whom the world would be a far less fascinating place.

WHERE TO STAY TO SEE ELEPHANTS

Kenya

Elephant Watch Camp, Samburu National Reserve
The premier place to stay to view some of the most researched elephants in Africa. Perched on the sand banks of the Ewaso Nyiro River the camp, which is eco-friendly has been specially constructed for comfort and coolness, accommodates a maximum of ten guests with its wide and breezy desert tents. Everything about Elephant Watch Camp is a feast for the senses.

E: info@elephantwatchsafaris.com | W: www.elephantwatchsafaris.com
T: (254 20)334868 | Best times to visit: Any time

Amboselli Serena
Probably the most famous place to see elephants in the shadow of Mount Kilimanjaro. Sensitively located and built from ecologically sympathetic materials, its architectural shapes, style, textures and colours reflect the true essence of the African bush. The rooms (96), each have an uninterrupted view over the ever-changing vistas of the African plains.

E: cro@serena.co.ke | W: www.serenahotels.com
Best times to visit: Jan, Feb, Mar and Oct, Nov, Dec

Namibia

Damaraland Camp
Damaraland Camp is a rare venture which integrates communities, the environment and sustainable wildlife and is rated as the most successful eco-tourism venture in Namibia. All nine tents have valley views and each has en suite facilities and a covered veranda. A feature of the camp is a stunning rock plunge pool tucked away in a mini gorge behind the camp.

E: info@nts.com.na | www.wilderness-safaris.com
T: (264 61) 274500 | Best times to visit: Apr-Dec best for elephants

Botswana

Dumatau Camp (Dumatau *is a local word meaning* 'where the lion roars')
The Linyanti Reserve consists of 125,000 hectares of prime wildlife countryside in Northern Botswana. Located just east of the source of the Savuti Channel. Accommodation is in nine luxurious, raised, tented rooms under thatch with en suite facilities. There are a number of hides in the area which give guests the opportunity to observe and photograph animals close up in their natural environment without disturbance.

E: info@nts.com.na | www.wilderness-safaris.com
T: (264 61) 274500 | Best times to visit: Mar-Dec

Sri Lanka

Deer Park Hotel (Minneria National Park)
Located within the Cultural Triangle of Ceylon, along the banks of the Giritale Reservoir, Deer Park is about 4hours from Colombo, the capital of Sri Lanka. This eco-sensitive resort takes its name from the tropical jungle — once the private hunting grounds of ancient kings — in which it was built. There are 77 cottages, 61 of which feature open-air garden bathrooms and outdoor showers.

E: reservations@angsana.com | www.coloursofangsana.com
T: (94 027) 224 6470 | Best times to visit: any, particularly Sept, Oct and Feb, Mar.

JF Tours
Excellent all round personally tailored transportation and arrangement of tours throughout Sri Lanka.

E: jft@slt.lk | T: (94 011) 2589402, 2587996, 2583387

Name of Photo: Splatter
Page: 64/65
Fondly known as 'Splatter', this image of a bull elephant spraying mud was taken using a remote camera and won the Animal Behaviour category of the BBC Wildlife Photographer of the Year competition. The camera with an attached infra red trigger and wide-angle lens was buried at the edge of the mud wallow. Upon hearing the click of the shutter button, the elephant promptly flung a trunk full of mud at the camera creating the final image. (Southern Africa, Canon EOS 5, Canon 17-35mm lens, Fuji Provia 100 film, Canon LC-3 remote trigger, 1/320th at f8).

Name of Photo: Asian Elephant Family at Sunrise
Page: 6/7
A good professional trick to achieving a perfect silhouette is to spot meter from the brightest part of the scene. This fools the lightmeter of the camera into believing that the scene is brighter than it really is. Consequently, the camera decreases the aperture with the effect of darkening the subject sufficiently to produce no detail. (Sri Lanka, Canon EOS 1Ds, Canon 70-200 f2.8L lens, 1/250th sec at f4, ISO 50).

Name of Photo: Close Encounter
Page: Front cover
The sense of power of the advancing bull elephant makes this an unforgettable image, especially as this image was captured by lying flat in front of the elephant. The image was taken in the full glare of the midday sun as the elephants' path could be predicted as they made their way to the water's edge. To reduce the harshness of the sun a 81A filter was used. (Southern Africa, Canon EOS 1V HS, Canon 17-35mm lens, Fuji Velvia film, 1/250th sec. at f8).

Name of Photo: Mr Chips Feeding
Page: 22
An abstract of a great character called Mr Chips, affectionately named by a good friend of ours due to his chip-shaped tusks. The sense of power and magnificence was created by utilising a slow shutter speed of 1/20th sec at f18. This effectively blurred the motion, lending an atmospheric and novel feel to the image. (Southern Africa, Canon EOS 1Ds, Canon 70-200 f2.8L IS lens, ISO 100)

Name of Photo: Sri Lankan Perehera
Page: 89
This image documents some of the sights and sounds of a perehera (a religious festival) in Sri Lanka. It was a real challenge to capture the mood of the scene. Despite being taken at night, a flash was not used, instead a slow shutter speed allowed us to pick out details and some interesting effects of the procession following the elephant. (Sri Lanka, Canon EOS 1Ds, Tamron 28-75mm Di lens, 1/13th sec. at f2.8, ISO 320)